First Facts™

Positively Pets

Caring for Your Rabbit

by Sarah Maass

Consultant:
Jennifer Zablotny, DVM
Member, American Veterinary Medical Association

Capstone press®
Mankato, Minnesota

First Facts is published by Capstone Press,
151 Good Counsel Drive, P.O. Box 669, Mankato, Minnesota 56002.
www.capstonepress.com

Library of Congress Cataloging-in-Publication Data
Maass, Sarah.
    Caring for Your Rabbit / by Sarah Maass.
    p. cm.—(First Facts. Positively pets)
    Summary: "Simple text and photographs discuss ways to take care of pet rabbits"
—Provided by publisher.
    Includes bibliographical references (p. 23) and index.
    ISBN-13: 978-0-7368-6389-6 (hardcover)
    ISBN-10: 0-7368-6389-3 (hardcover)
1. Rabbits—Juvenile literature. I. Title. II. Series: Pet care (Mankato, Minn.)
SF453.2.M22 2007
636.932'2—dc22   2005036374

Editorial Credits
Mari Schuh, editor; Bobbi J. Wyss, designer; Kim Brown, illustrator; Kelly Garvin,
    photo researcher/photo editor

Photo Credits
Capstone Press/Karon Dubke, cover, 5, 6, 7, 9, 13, 14, 15, 17, 21
Getty Images Inc./Photonica/Kristina Williamson, 18–19
Minden Pictures/Foto Natura/Edwin Giesbers, 20
Norvia Behling, 10–11

Capstone Press thanks Pet Expo and River Hills Pet Care Hospital in Mankato, Minnesota,
for assistance with photo shoots.

The author dedicates this book to her mother, Maria Lindberg of Blue Earth, Minnesota,
who has raised angora rabbits for more than 30 years.

1 2 3 4 5 6 11 10 09 08 07 06

Table of Contents

So You Want to Own a Rabbit?

Rabbits hop in their **hutches** at the local pet store. You love to touch their soft fur. You really want a pet rabbit. But are you ready for the **responsibility?**

Learn more about rabbits and how to take care of them. Then a rabbit can be your healthy pet for many years.

Supplies to Buy

Your rabbit will need some supplies. Rabbits need a hutch. Put it indoors if you can. Buy rabbit food, bowls for food and water, toys, and bedding.

Your rabbit has soft and tender feet. If you buy a wire hutch, put a rug or cardboard on the hutch's floor. Then your rabbit's feet won't get sore.

Your Rabbit at Home

Rabbits are playful and curious. Every day, let your rabbit out to hop, jump, and play. Rabbits love to chew on things. Keep your rabbit away from electrical cords and house plants.

Be gentle with your rabbit. Pick it up carefully. An adult can show you how to safely hold a rabbit.

My teeth keep growing my whole life. Chewing on things helps wear them down. Give me things to chew on like sticks and wooden toys.

Your Rabbit with Other Pets

Your rabbit will likely be shy or scared around other pets. Never leave your rabbit alone with another pet. Your rabbit could get hurt.

Rabbits usually enjoy making friends with other rabbits. But it's best to let them get used to each other outside of their own hutches.

Feeding Your Rabbit

Your hungry rabbit needs fresh food, hay, and water every day. Feed your rabbit food **pellets** that are made just for him.

Rabbits can eat some other food too. Carrots and parsley are good vegetables for them.

Iceberg lettuce, rhubarb, corn, and potatoes can make me sick. Check with my vet before giving me new foods.

Cleaning

Rabbits like to be clean and dry.
They lick themselves to stay clean.
Brush your pet at least once a week
so it doesn't swallow loose hair.

Rabbits need clean hutches. Help your pet stay healthy by keeping its hutch clean. Replace old bedding with new bedding every day.

A Visit to the Vet

Your rabbit should visit a **veterinarian** at least once a year. The vet is an animal doctor who will check your rabbit's body.

When your rabbit is about six months old, it can be **spayed** or **neutered** to keep it from having bunnies. This operation makes your rabbit calmer and healthier.

Your Rabbit's Life

Good food, care, and exercise will keep your rabbit healthy. It may live 8 to 12 years. Take good care of your rabbit. You can have many years to play together!

The oldest living rabbit is a Netherlands dwarf rabbit named Sniffles. Sniffles was born in February 1991 and lives in Knoxville, Tennessee.

Wild Relatives!

You might have watched your rabbit dig up its bedding or hay. Wild rabbits dig a lot too. Many rabbits dig burrows and tunnels. These underground homes keep rabbits safe and warm. Make a space in your rabbit's hutch where it can safely dig and scratch.

Decode Your Rabbit's Behavior

- Rabbits sometimes eat their own droppings. If you see this happen, don't worry. Rabbits get extra vitamins from their droppings.

- You might hear your rabbit make a loud thump with its hind feet. This is your rabbit's way to warn you or other rabbits of possible danger. Your rabbit also might be scared or mad.

- Rabbits softly grind their teeth when they are content. This is a rabbit's way of purring like a cat. If your rabbit loudly grinds its teeth, it might be in pain.

Glossary

hutch (HUHCH)—a place where rabbits or other small pets live; hutches should be big enough so that rabbits can move around.

neuter (NOO-tur)—to operate on a male animal so it is unable to produce young

pellet (PEL-it)—a small hard ball of compressed food

responsibility (ri-spon-suh-BIL-uh-tee)—a duty or job

spay (SPAY)—to operate on a female animal so it is unable to produe young

veterinarian (vet-ur-uh-NER-ee-uhn)—a doctor who treats sick or injured animals; veterinarians also help animals stay healthy.

Read More

Klingel, Cynthia Fitterer, and Robert B. Noyed. *Rabbits.* Wonder Books. Chanhassen, Minn.: Child's World, 2001.

Macken, JoAnn Early. *Rabbits.* Let's Read about Pets. Milwaukee: Weekly Reader Early Learning Library, 2004.

Spilsbury, Louise, and Richard Spilsbury. *Rabbits.* Keeping Pets. Chicago: Heinemann Library, 2006.

Internet Sites

FactHound offers a safe, fun way to find Internet sites related to this book. All of the sites on FactHound have been researched by our staff.

Here's how:

1. Visit *www.facthound.com*

2. Choose your grade level.

3. Type in this book ID **0736863893** for age-appropriate sites. You may also browse subjects by clicking on letters, or by clicking on pictures and words.

4. Click on the **Fetch It** button.

FactHound will fetch the best sites for you!

Index